*Certification Model
for Professional
School Media Personnel*

Certification Model for Professional School Media Personnel

AMERICAN ASSOCIATION
OF SCHOOL LIBRARIANS

Certification Model for Professional School Media Personnel

CERTIFICATION OF
SCHOOL MEDIA SPECIALISTS COMMITTEE

AMERICAN ASSOCIATION
OF SCHOOL LIBRARIANS

A DIVISION OF THE
AMERICAN LIBRARY ASSOCIATION

AMERICAN LIBRARY ASSOCIATION
Chicago 1976

ISBN 0-8389-3179-0

Copyright © 1976 by the American Library Association
All rights reserved. No part of this publication may be reproduced in any form without permission in writing from the publisher, except by a reviewer who may quote brief passages in a review.

Printed in the United States of America

Contents

PREFACE	vii
INTRODUCTION	1
PLANNING STATE CERTIFICATION DESIGNS	3
CANDIDATE ASSESSMENT PROCESS	5
AREAS OF COMPETENCIES	8
APPENDIXES:	
A. STUDY OF CERTIFICATION REQUIREMENTS	19
B. IMPACT OF NATIONAL ORGANIZATIONS ON CERTIFICATION	21
C. COMMITTEE MEMBERS	27
GLOSSARY	29
BIBLIOGRAPHY	31

Preface

This model on media professional certification has been developed over the past year with a grant from the J. Morris Jones—World Book Encyclopedia, American Library Association Goals Award. The sixteen-member committee, charged with the responsibility of writing the model, was able to conduct a very thorough examination of existing certification practices. Thus, a more comprehensive model for certification practices, reflective of the input of concerned members throughout the country, was ultimately developed.

Prior to the review of the working draft of the model, the committee developed two working drafts. The original working draft was written by a ten-member subcommittee during a three-day meeting at Millersville State College in Millersville, Pennsylvania. This draft was then reviewed by the total committee, and their reactions were subsequently incorporated into the second working draft. During work sessions in Chicago, Midwinter 1975, the review model was finalized and, in February 1975, 431 copies of the model were mailed to a representative sampling of persons across the country for their reactions. Groups which received the review model were American Association of School Librarian committee chairpersons, presidents of state media associations, selected deans and faculty members of media educational programs, state certification officers, state school media supervisors, selected district media supervisors, and seven other professional associations. Approximately 46 percent of those polled responded to the review draft. Following is an analysis of these responses:

	YES	NO
Does the model reflect current and future practices?	152	10
Is its organization logical?	162	12
Need any additional items be added?	86	68

In addition to these copies of the model which were mailed to various persons and organizations, the model was also discussed before the Colorado Media Convention, the Connecticut School Library Association and Connecticut Audiovisual Education Association Joint Spring Conference, the New England Regional Media Conference, and the conference sponsored by the Michigan Association for Media in Education and Wayne State University. Included in these sessions were representatives of building, district, and state levels as well as colleges and universities whose comments and reactions were also recorded.

Later, another subcommittee met on June 6, 7, 8, 1975, in Louisville, Kentucky, to revise the model according to the combined input of these respondents. Obviously, the final product has been strengthened by such diverse analysis.

To all who assisted in any way in the formulation of this model, and especially to Field Enterprises, the committee wishes to express its sincere gratitude.

Introduction

In a rapidly changing society, the relevance and validity of current practices are constantly being challenged. Within the field of education, the knowledge explosion and technological developments have created the need for new staffing patterns in our schools. Since the emphasis is on learning rather than teaching, the role of the school media program is of major importance. The unified media concept has evolved into a program which provides a full range of materials, accompanying technology, and services to meet the inspirational, informational, and recreational needs of students and members of the instructional team. The media program encourages students to explore on their own, or in small or large groups, areas of interest which have been aroused either by the curriculum or by personal experiences.

The educational preparation required of persons working in this type of environment is different from that of the traditional librarian, audiovisualist, and educational television personnel. A wide variety of competencies are needed by media professionals so that they may satisfy the demands placed upon the school media program. They need competencies derived from educational programs in general education, professional education, and media specialization.

Presently, there is no nationally recognized process for certifying school media professionals. Certification requirements are established by the individual states and vary greatly from one state to another. Where reciprocity exists, problems have been identified concerning its implementation. The requirements of state and regional accrediting associations are not generally expressive of media program demands.

In light of all these differences, the American Association of School Librarians established a committee to study and investigate current certification practices and how these practices affect media personnel (see appendix A). Numerous agencies are requesting direction in planning, developing, and implementing certification practices to meet the changing demands identified in the media field. It is envisioned that a cooperatively developed school media certification model will assist in providing direction in the development of state and regional practices. The model shall in no way be prescriptive; it should be the responsibility of state groups and others to adapt the model to their own individual needs.

Just as certification practice needs to be examined and upgraded, so do the programs being offered by academic institutions preparing school media professionals. Both need re-evaluating to insure that a unified media approach, which provides the types of personnel demanded in the school media program, is in existence. The model indicates the desirability of continual and ongoing professional growth and development of media personnel. Certification practices should provide for and promote continuous progress to advanced levels of certification.

Individuals from all areas of the educational community were involved in planning and writing the model contained in this document. Others from across the country provided valuable assistance in reviewing the model through its developmental stages. Therefore, the model was not designed in isolation but represents the views of many individuals and groups. The model should be under constant revision to insure its usefulness. It will be necessary for future revisions to reflect current trends, developments, and needs. Further study and investigation also need to be undertaken in the area of licensing and certifying media paraprofessionals.

Planning State Certification Designs

The certification pattern for media specialists should be compatible with the practices and procedures for other educational personnel within a state or area. Committees or task forces should be established to plan the certification design. These groups should be broadly representative of media specialists, professional organizations, state departments of education, and institutions of higher education.

It is recognized that there should be more than one possible point of entry for media professionals. In addition, there should be more than one level of certification for media professionals. The point of entry into the school media profession is the first professional certificate granted to the candidate in the media area. Certain candidates may enter the ranks as a certificated professional with minimal or basic attainment of the competencies identified in this document. Others may enter with a higher level of attainment. It is expected that there will be continuing professional development for all persons within the media field, regardless of the certification at entry. The certification design or pattern should provide recognition for the attainment of greater degrees of skill within the specified areas of competencies. Furthermore, competency requirements should reflect different levels of responsibility. The design should also provide mobility between and within building and district level positions.

Beginning level media professionals should have basic competencies in all areas identified in this document. The entry levels and the certification levels should be based on the degree of capability attained within each competency area. The methods of measuring this attainment may vary from state to state. Some possible methods of measurement are suggested in the next section, Candidate Assessment Process.

Incentive programs should be provided which encourage professionals to strive for higher degrees of capabilities. The following methods can be incorporated in programs of continuing education:

1. Formal courses or seminars
2. Formal courses leading to advanced degrees
3. Workshops or in-service programs
4. Specially designed programs to meet identified needs
5. Planned independent study
6. Research
7. Practicum
8. Work experience in different settings (another school, district center, teaching)
9. Planned visitations

Continuing educational experiences can be provided for in numerous settings, including school, district, or regional levels; institutions of higher learning; or any combination of these.

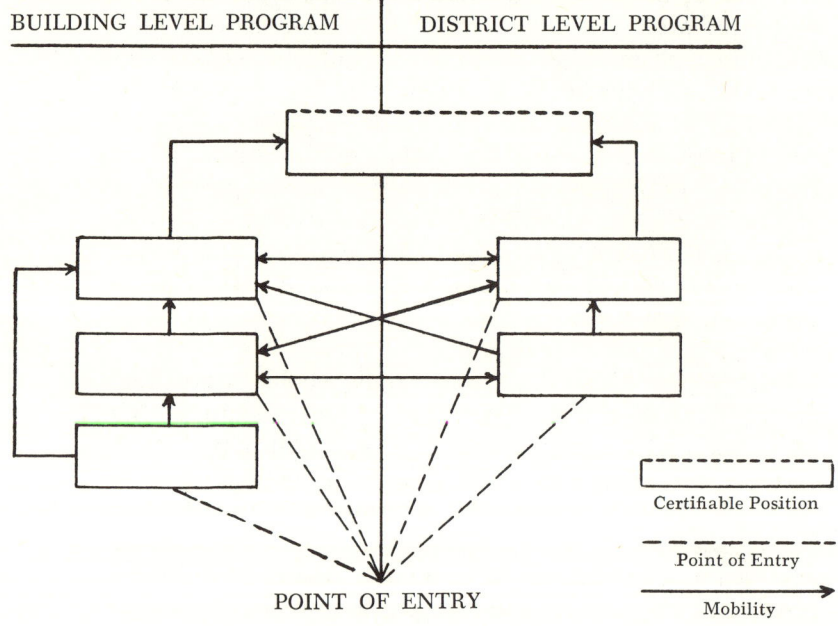

STEPS IN CERTIFICATION PROCESS

Candidate Assessment Process

After developing its own certification design, each state will need to establish the process for determining whether or not candidates qualify for a certificate and at which level. The process should be compatible with the process utilized for other educational professionals, such as teachers, administrators, reading specialists, and counselors.

Although this document places emphasis on competencies, there are numerous strategies for assessing candidate qualifications and granting certificates. This model suggests that the use of a combination of assessment techniques is a more valid approach.

Determining competencies or proficiencies should be an integral part of any evaluation process. This does not imply that strictly competency-based certification should be utilized by all states. Where other patterns are established, the competencies necessary should be identified and utilized in evaluating the candidate and/or the educational program developed for preparing candidates for entry into the media profession and for advancement to higher levels of certification.

The designing of the assessment process should involve representatives from the various groups within the educational community, such as media professionals, other teaching personnel, administrators, and professional organizations, including media associations, personnel from state departments of education, and media educators. The assessment process for certification should be designed to include the following points:

1. The criteria used for assessment should be publicly stated and made known to the candidate at the point of entry into the media education program.
2. The assessment process, within defined levels of entry, should be consistent for all candidates using equivalent criteria and comparable procedures.

3. The assessment process should be analytical and objective—using a variety of procedures which will diagnose strengths and deficiencies and yield a candidate profile.
4. The assessment process should consider a variety of collected data which illustrate the candidate's behavior and performance in the affective, cognitive, and psychomotor domains.
5. The entry level assessment should be viewed only as a measure of the candidate's current qualifications.
6. The process for candidates to qualify and be reassessed for more advanced certification levels should be established.
7. A grievance procedure should be established and made available to the candidate.
8. A continuous review and revision of the assessment process should reflect current practices and needs of education and media programs.
9. The assessment process for certification should have well-established guidelines covering such factors as:
   a. Definition of certification levels
   b. Length of validity of certificate
   c. Requirements (regional and state) including liberal arts, general education, professional education, and specialized courses unique to the needs of the media field
   d. Guidelines for responsibilities at each level of certification
   e. Application process for each level of certification
   f. Requirements for renewal
   g. Information concerning reciprocity
   h. Grandfather clause (Provision could be made for providing a process whereby persons presently holding professional certificates are not required to meet the new requirements. However, these individuals should participate in opportunities which will assist in keeping their professional preparation current and relevant.)
   i. Clear identification of the agency which has the responsibility for examining a candidate's competencies

10. The assessment process for certification should provide various data gathering strategies or techniques. Strategies to be considered include:
    a. Rating of performance(s) in live-role situations under direct and systematic observation
    b. Evaluative reports regarding performance
    c. Appraisal of the tangible evidence or product of role performance
    d. Achievement examinations
    e. Appraisal of personal attributes
    f. Special performance tests in live or simulated environments to evaluate proficiency in a single competency
    g. Media education institutional recommendations
    h. Transcript analysis

Areas of Competencies

The certification of professional media personnel by state agencies or their designated representatives is based upon the premise that the candidate for certification has achieved a required level of proficiency. What constitutes any one level of proficiency must be based upon the identification of those competencies necessary to guarantee accountable performance in the field.

A concerted effort has been made within the school media profession to identify the responsibilities and appropriate competencies of the school media professional. National studies and projects, such as the Jobs in Media, Hamreus-Edling Project, the School Library Manpower Project, and the work of the two major national associations in the media field—the American Association of School Librarians and the Association of Educational Communications and Technology—have provided a foundation for this document. Therefore, although the specific terminology may differ in some instances, the commonalities reflect a general consensus within the school media profession.

The seven major competencies here delineated are those which are needed by all media professionals. They should serve as a model from which state departments of certification can proceed and should in no way inhibit the expansion of these competencies into a more inclusive coverage.

Each of the seven major competencies is described with its definition and is then subdivided into more discrete statements. Candidates for certification will need to demonstrate proficiency in all the stated competencies; however, the degree of required competency will vary depending upon the educational level obtained, job assignment, and responsibilities. Certification procedures should recognize variations in the levels of degree of competency attainment, and the requirements for these variations must be clearly defined. The seven areas of competencies within this model are:

1. Relation of Media to Instructional Systems
2. Administration of Media Programs
3. Selection of Media
4. Utilization of Media
5. Production of Media
6. Research and Evaluation
7. Leadership and Professionalism

1. RELATION OF MEDIA TO INSTRUCTIONAL SYSTEMS

Relating media to instructional systems is the ability to apply the principles of learning and learning theory by assisting individuals or groups in the pursuit of informational objectives.

The candidate will demonstrate the ability to:
a. Participate, as a member of the educational team, in the design and continual development of the curriculum
b. Determine goals for the media program as an integral part of the educational program of the school and district
c. Plan learning activities and opportunities that will enable students to assume an increasing amount of responsibility for planning, undertaking, and assessing their own learning
d. Analyze learner characteristics, such as various abilities, interests, needs, and learning styles
e. Recommend alternative learning environments
f. Participate in the evaluation and modification of teaching/learning designs

2. ADMINISTRATION OF MEDIA PROGRAMS

Administration is the ability to develop and implement media programs which facilitate the achievement of the educational goals, including the process of management of the media and human resources.

The candidate will demonstrate the ability to:
a. Assess the current status of the media program in terms of district, state, regional, and national guidelines and to establish short- and long-range plans
b. Apply the principles of management to the administration of the media program
c. Initiate, develop, and implement policies and procedures for the operation of the media center
d. Establish procedures for effective and efficient acquisition, processing, cataloging, distribution, and maintenance of materials and equipment
e. Invite and accept suggestions from students and faculty about the services the program provides
f. Maintain an effective public relations program which communicates to students, teachers, administrative staff, parents, and the public the vital contribution of the media program to learning
g. Plan and conduct in-service experiences for media staff and school faculty
h. Utilize the contributions and abilities of each media center staff member and provide for staff development
i. Prepare, justify, and administer the media program budget
j. Design, develop, and write proposals for the acquisition of local, state, and federal funds to support and extend media programs
k. Participate in the planning, arrangement, and utilization and development of media facilities which will support the objectives of the media program and the instructional program
l. Prepare statistical records and written reports of the media program
m. Implement policies and procedures for the purpose of maintaining control systems for media, equipment, and facilities

n. Identify and interpret legislation which affects the media program
o. Apply principles of school law to the administration of the media program
p. Establish job specifications and apply principles of personnel management

3. SELECTION OF MEDIA

The selection of media is the ability to apply basic principles of evaluating and selecting media to support the instructional program.

The candidate will demonstrate the ability to:
a. Develop and implement criteria for evaluating and selecting a variety of materials and equipment
b. Build a collection of bibliographic aids and tools and other sources to provide current reviews and information about materials and equipment
c. Establish and administer processes and procedures for preview, evaluation, selection, and acquisition of materials and equipment
d. Provide teaching and learning resources to support teacher and student objectives
e. Develop selection policies which meet curricular, informational, and recreational needs and conform to the appropriate legal requirements

4. UTILIZATION OF MEDIA

The utilization of media is the ability to assist faculty and students in the use of the school media program which enhances the learning process. A thorough knowledge of media is essential for promoting its effective use.

The candidate will demonstrate the ability to:
   a. Teach skills in the retrieval and utilization of materials and equipment to students and teachers
   b. Assist teachers and students in identifying, obtaining, and adapting media to meet special needs
   c. Recommend and apply to teachers the application of media in various formats which can assist in the accomplishment of specific learning objectives
   d. Provide guidance in reading, listening, and viewing experiences for students and teachers
   e. Provide specific information and resources in response to reference requests

5. PRODUCTION OF MEDIA

The production of media is the ability to plan, design, and produce materials to supplement those available through other channels.

The candidate will demonstrate the ability to:
a. Operate production equipment
b. Evaluate and select production equipment and supplies
c. Produce media for specified learning objectives which utilize the basic principles of design
d. Establish and apply criteria for decision making concerning the desirability of locally produced media as opposed to available commercially produced media
e. Design production facilities and establish basic routines for the operation of those facilities
f. Instruct and supervise others in media design and production

6. RESEARCH AND EVALUATION

Research and evaluation are the ability to interpret and apply recorded research and evaluative data applicable to media programs, and to design and implement studies relative to the media center program when there is an identified need.

The candidate will demonstrate the ability to:
a. Apply the principles of research to the development and advancement of the media program
b. Determine the need for conducting research activities to support the goals of the media program
c. Design and adapt an identified research study for the development and advancement of the media program
d. Gather data for identified research study related to the media program
e. Analyze and evaluate information gathered in specified research studies of media programs
f. Apply the specified research findings for the improvement of the media program
g. Disseminate research information
h. Develop a plan of assessment and evaluation of the media program based upon stated objectives

7. LEADERSHIP AND PROFESSIONALISM

Leadership and professionalism are the ability to conceive, synthesize, promote, and direct media programs reflecting a commitment to professional ethics.

The candidate will demonstrate the ability to:
a. Practice effective interpersonal relationships within the educational community
b. Recognize the components of the community structure and utilize the special knowledge, abilities, and resources of people and institutions within the community
c. Provide and protect within the existing legal framework the right of access for faculty and students
d. Engage in self-evaluation to identify the areas of need for continuing education and professional growth
e. Participate in district, county, regional, state, and national organizations
f. Engage in research and publication activities

Appendix A

STUDY OF CERTIFICATION REQUIREMENTS

A study of existing certification requirements for school building level librarians or media specialists in all fifty states and the District of Columbia shows a wide diversification of specified credit hours, courses, or areas, as well as media titles identifying media personnel. Certification requirements for the school librarian or media specialist are confusing and unstructured; some states are most strict in the requirements while others are not yet as well organized. The wide range of credit hours existing among the fifty states (some of which have multiple systems) and the District of Columbia can be illustrated by the following data (as of January 1975):

- 11 states require less than 18 semester hours in media education
- 19 states require 18 semester hours
- 5 states require more than 18 semester hours
- 14 states require 24 semester hours
- 3 states require more than 24 semester hours
- 20 states require 30 or more semester hours in media education

The number of titles for qualified school media personnel varies within each state, as well—from one basic title for all qualified personnel to seven different names or positions, depending on the program followed. The complexity of multititles *within* each state, depending on the number of media education credit hours received, is another dilemma. Three states do not spell out credit-hour requirements, courses, or areas; these states rely on the approved or accredited institution to determine the educational qualifications necessary for developing competent school media specialists.

Three states are presently involved in the competency-based approach for educating school media personnel. No credit hours are noted but the student is required to demonstrate competencies or proficiencies in specified areas of media education. Five states at present prescribe specified credit hours in which to develop the required competencies or proficiencies in stated areas. This type of certification is a combination of credit hours with competencies and can be called the credit-competency-combination or compromise. The competency-based approach is not entirely new, and a number of states are studying or considering this aspect of media education.

It can be safely said that no study of certification requirements can be completely current or up-to-date because of constant changing and updating by the states. It can be stated also that, at the present time, certification requirements for media personnel are lacking in uniformity of structure. The nearest common denominator is the fact that the states are trying to upgrade the educational requirements in library science, audiovisual, and professional education to produce competent media personnel who will be able to administer effective building level media programs.

Appendix B

IMPACT OF NATIONAL ORGANIZATIONS ON CERTIFICATION

AASL School Library Manpower Project*

This project is a direct result of the:

Standards for School Library Programs (ALA, 1960) which mandated the need for school media specialists to have a mastery of new concepts in the profession to meet the diversity of job responsibilities in school library programs, the proliferation of media, and their extensive use in library programs required by educational innovations.

Knapp School Libraries Demonstration Project which illustrated the need to seek new ways to recruit school library personnel; to study and implement more effective ways to educate them in their field of specialization; and to determine how these persons could be best utilized in education.

National Inventory of Library Needs (ALA, 1965) which revealed the special concerns of school librarianship in providing sufficient well-qualified personnel to insure quality library service in every school.

The School Library Manpower Project was implemented in three phases and extended from 1968 through 1974.

Phase I was devoted to an examination of educational change and its effect upon school librarianship. A significant outcome of this phase was the publication *School Library Personnel: Task Analysis Survey* (ALA, 1969). Six hundred and ninety-four outstanding school media programs were involved in the survey and the summary presents a picture of the kinds of tasks media specialists performed and how much time was spent on various tasks.

---

*See *Curriculum Alternatives: Experiments in School Library Media Education,* American Library Association, 1974. Phase I, pp. 3-8, presents a detailed overview of the *School Library Manpower Project* and its various phased components.

Anticipating that an in-depth analysis of the survey's findings would be necessary, a special Task Analysis Committee was appointed composed of ten members who represented a wide variety of position levels and disciplines in the fields of school librarianship, library education, library and education administration, technology, and public personnel.

In fulfilling its assignment to the Project, the Task Analysis Committee was charged with two major concerns—that of developing occupational definitions which would provide a career lattice approach for mobility within the positions, and, secondly, to identify in a series of statements the role and impact the definitions would have on the development of the six experimental programs during Phase II.

The four occupational definitions that resulted from the work of this committee were School Library Media Specialist, Head of the School Library Media Center, District School Library Media Director, and the School Library Media Technician. The major components of the occupational definitions included the nature and scope of the position, major duties, and the knowledges and abilities required for the position. The definitions were published in a 1971 Project publication, *Occupational Definitions for School Library Media Personnel.*

Coterminous with the development of the occupational definitions, an eleven-member Curriculum Content Committee was appointed to study the new definitions and to develop objectives and recommend guidelines for new curriculum programs in school library media education.

The Curriculum Content Committee was representative of schools of education, library school administration, undergraduate and graduate library and audiovisual education programs, district school library media supervisors, practicing elementary and secondary school librarians, and recent library school graduates. Through its discussions and deliberations, the Curriculum Content Committee was cognizant of the broad implications the recommendations would have for the Phase II experimental programs and for library education as a whole. Following the agreement on objectives for a school library media education program, the committee analyzed the occupational definitions and identified "Major Areas of Competencies for the Education of the School Library Media Specialist." The seven major areas of competencies identified were Media, Human Behavior, Learning and Learning Environment, Planning and Evaluation, Management, Research, and Professionalism. Each major competency area was defined and supported by a series of behavioral objectives. The study of the Curriculum Content Committee was further detailed in its report, "Suggestions for Curriculum Content Within Major Areas of Competencies."

Phase II of the School Library Manpower Project was designed to build upon the results and recommendations of Phase I. Its primary goal was to provide six relevant experimental program models in school library media education and intelligent responses to the needs identified in Phase I.

The six institutions selected by the Project Advisory Committee received $100,000 each to develop, implement, and evaluate new curriculum design and innovative approaches for the education of professional school library media personnel. An additional $2,000 planning grant was awarded to each institution to support staff development activities prior to the implementation of the programs. The institutions approved for awards were Arizona State University, Tempe; Auburn University, Alabama; Mankato State College, Minnesota; Millersville State College, Pennsylvania; University of Denver, Colorado; and the University of Michigan, Ann Arbor. Each experimental program began some phase of operation in September 1971.

During the two years of experimentation, each of the six programs—one at the undergraduate level, one at the post-master's level, one at both the undergraduate and graduate levels, and three at the graduate level—pursued its own program objectives explicated for training personnel identified in one or more of the occupational definitions. Each program was involved also in research and evaluation relevant to its own unique objectives. The Project staff, with the assistance of each institution and the Human Resources Research Organization, developed a plan to coordinate the research and evaluation for all six programs.

Each of the experimental programs is explained in the document, *Curriculum Alternatives: Experiments in School Library Media Education* (1974). This report is useful as a summary of the important findings from each of the six experimental programs and can provide further evidence for the needed certification competencies for school library media specialists.

Phase III was developed to provide an assessment of the validity of the six experimental programs funded during Phase II and to give guidance for the future direction of school library media education programs. A second, and equally important goal, was to demonstrate the value of a quality-control system for the continued evaluation and improvement of education programs. The entire Phase III effort of the Project was devoted to obtaining quality-control feedback from program graduates.

The data-collecting instrument used was the Project publication, *Behavioral Requirements Analysis Checklist,* developed during Phase II. It was used during the evaluation to identify rather precisely those tasks performed by program graduates. This instrument, coupled with a series of evaluation-related questions, provided the evaluation tool needed to show the degree to which the experimental programs had prepared graduates to work competently in the field.

A particularly important outcome of the Project was its impact on efforts in some states to revise certification guidelines for school library media educational programs. The models and materials developed during the Project provided suggestions as to how state certification programs for school library media personnel could be modified. A full report of the evaluation carried out during Phase III of the Project can be found in *Evaluation of Alternative Curricula: Approaches to School Library Media Education.*

AECT CERTIFICATION TASK FORCE REPORT

In 1971, a task force was established by the Association for Educational Communications and Technology to work on problems pertaining to the certification of educational communications and technology personnel. Eight meetings of the task force were held along with three hearings and reviews over a two-year period of time. Their relevant specific recommendations are:

1. That serious consideration be given to the approval and publication of these guidelines;
2. That a vehicle be established whereby continuing study can be made of the impact of the guidelines in the field for further revision and refinement;
3. That a vehicle be established to develop guidelines for the certification of educational communications and technology personnel graduating from two-year programs;
4. That a vehicle be established to study the problems of "certifying" aides, as defined in this report; and
5. That a vehicle be established to study the role of the "technician" in instructional program development.

As the task force notes:

Standards for the certification of educational communications and technology personnel were first established by the Association for Educational Communications and Technology (then the Department of Audiovisual Instruction) in 1969. As the profession of education and the educational communications and technology field have developed, the need for a rationale on which to base a certification plan for the field, as well as for the plan itself, have been assigned high priorities in the Association for Educational Communications and Technology. Previous work undertaken by its Commission on the Professional Education of Media Specialists (PEMS) formed the basis for the further work undertaken here by the Certification Task Force. The concurrent work of the staffs of AECT's Jobs in Instructional Media (JIMS), the Hamreus-Edling Media Guidelines Project, and the School Library Manpower Project provided an essential data base.

The report then presents the need for certification of educational communications and technology personnel employed in schools and colleges and for which agencies these guidelines will be useful.

The guidelines are competency-based and define three levels of competency: (1) entry or aide positions; (2) middle or technician positions; and (3) advanced or specialist positions. Within each specialization they have identified nine basic media functions:

1. Organization management
2. Personnel management
3. Research/theory
4. Design
5. Production
6. Evaluation/selection
7. Support/supply
8. Utilization
9. Utilization/dissemination

They then further subdivide the specializations into: (1) Media Management-Technicians; (2) Media Management-Specialists; (3) Media Product Development-Technicians; (4) Media Product Development-Specialists; (5) Instructional Program Development-Technicians; and (6) Instructional Program Development-Specialists. Under each specialization, the general necessary competencies are listed. Appended to the document is a lengthy detailed list of specific competencies for each general competency area.

Appendix C

COMMITTEE MEMBERS

*DAVID R. BENDER, *Chairperson*
  Assistant Director, School Media Office
  Maryland State Department of Education
  Baltimore, Maryland

*DONALD C. ADCOCK
  Director of Library Services
  School District #41
  Glen Ellyn, Illinois

*JOSEPH F. BLAKE
  Chairman, Department of Educational Media
  Millersville State College
  Millersville, Pennsylvania

*REBECCA J. EARLS
  Consultant for School Media Services
  Kentucky Department of Education
  Frankfort, Kentucky

*ANN Y. FRANKLIN
  Library Consultant
  Jefferson County Public Schools
  Louisville, Kentucky

*THOMAS L. HART
  Assistant Professor, Library Science
  Florida State University
  Tallahassee, Florida

MARION HENRY
  Director, Learning Resource Center
  Prairie View A. & M. University
  Prairie View, Texas

*GRACE HIGHTOWER
  Associate Director for Media Field Services
  Georgia Department of Education
  Atlanta, Georgia

LESLIE H. JANKE
  Chairman, Department of Librarianship
  San Jose State College
  San Jose, California
B. EUGENE KOSKEY
  Associate Director
  Center for Instructional Media and Program Development
  University of Wisconsin Center System
  Madison, Wisconsin
*ANNA MARY LOWREY
  Assistant Professor
  School of Information and Library Studies
  State University of New York at Buffalo
  Buffalo, New York
*LOTSEE P. SMITH
  Assistant Professor, College of Education
  University of New Mexico
  Albuquerque, New Mexico
DIANA L. SPIRT
  Professor of Library Science
  Long Island University
  Greenvale, New York
SARA K. SRYGLEY
  Professor of Library Science
  Florida State University
  Tallahassee, Florida
*KENNETH E. VANCE
  Assistant Dean, School of Library Science
  The University of Michigan
  Ann Arbor, Michigan

Ex Officio Members

*HELEN LLOYD
  Associate Professor, School of Library Science
  University of Michigan
  Ann Arbor, Michigan
*LUOUIDA PHILLIPS
  Executive Secretary
  American Association of School Librarians
  Chicago, Illinois

   *Design Subcommittee

Glossary

Much of the confusion in the educational field regarding the terms used in the media program stems from duplication of usage, changing characteristics, and nonstandard definitions. The following list of terms is included as a clarification of the terms used in this publication.

Director of district media program
A media professional with appropriate certification and advanced managerial, administrative, and supervisory competencies who qualifies for an administrative or supervisory position.

District media program
The media program that is conducted at the school district level through an administrative subunit.

Head of school media program
A media specialist with managerial competencies who is designated as responsible for the media program at the individual school level. Qualifications vary with such factors as the size of the school, size of media staff, and type of program.

Instructional system(s)
An integrated group of program components organized to accomplish stated objectives.

Media
Print and nonprint forms of communications and their accompanying technology.

Media professional
Any media person who qualifies by training and position to make professional judgments and to delineate and maintain media programs or program components. Media professionals may include media specialists, television or film producers, instructional developers, radio station managers, and technical processing (cataloging) specialists whose duties and responsibilities are professional in nature.

Point of entry
The point of entry into the profession is the first professional certificate granted to a candidate.

Practicum
A field experience involving the practical application of previously learned concepts and techniques in an operational situation.

School media center
An area or system of areas in the school where a full range of information sources, associated equipment, and services from media staff are accessible to students, school personnel, and the school community.

School media program
The media program for a school conducted through an administrative subunit.

Bibliography

"A Proposal for an Integrated Competency-Based School Media Endorsement Program for the State of New Mexico." Mimeographed. Albuquerque, N. M.: Univ. of Albuquerque, 1973.

Ahlers, Eleanor E., and Wieman, Jean B., comps. "School Library Media Supervisor Competencies—A Cyclic Design for Development." Seattle: Univ. of Washington, School of Librarianship, n.d.

Case, Robert M., and Lowrey, Anna Mary, eds. *Behavioral Requirements Analysis Checklist: A Compilation of Competency-Based Job Functions and Task Statements for School Library Media Personnel.* School Library Manpower Project, American Association of School Librarians. Chicago: American Library Assoc., 1973.

———. *Curriculum Alternatives: Experiments in School Library Media Education.* School Library Manpower Project, American Association of School Librarians. Chicago: American Library Assoc., 1974.

———. *Occupational Definitions for School Library Media Personnel.* Phase I. School Library Manpower Project, American Association of School Librarians. Chicago: American Library Assoc., 1971.

Central Washington Consortium Preparation Program for Building Level Library Media Specialists. Yakima, Washington: Central Washington Consortium for Certification of School Library Media Specialists, 1974.

"Certification and Accreditation." *Audiovisual Instruction*, Vol. 19, no. 9 (Nov. 1974).

Certification/Endorsement Program for Library–Media Specialists. Kelso, Washington: Southwest Washington Consortium for Certification of Library–Media Specialists, 1974.

Certification Requirements for Educational Media Personnel. Baltimore: Maryland State Department of Education, 1974.

Franklin, Ann Y. "School Library Certification Requirements." *School Library Journal*, 97:22-33 (Dec. 1972).

———. "School Library Certification Requirements— Phase II." *School Library Journal*, 98:17-29. (Dec. 1973).

———. "School Library Certification Requirements: 1974 Update." *School Library Journal,* 99:15-19 (Dec. 1974).

"Library Media Certification Competencies Survey." Mimeographed. MAME Certification Committee. Detroit: Wayne State Univ., n.d.

Media Programs: District and School. Chicago: American Library Assoc. and Washington, D.C.: Assoc. for Educational Communications and Technology, 1975.

Requirements for Instructional Media Endorsements. Rev. ed., Salt Lake City: Utah State Board of Education, 1972.

Southeastern Washington Consortium Endorsement Program for Building Level Library-Media Specialists. Walla Walla, Washington, 1974.

Standards & Guidelines for Approval of Institutions & Programs for Teacher Education (Competency-Based Program). Raleigh: North Carolina Department of Public Instruction, Division of Teacher Education, 1973.

Standards for School Media Programs. Chicago: American Library Assoc. and Washington, D.C.: National Education Association, 1969.

The Education Profession—1971-72—Part IV. "A Manpower Survey of the School Library Media Field." Washington, D.C.: U.S. Dept. of Health, Education, and Welfare, Education Division, Document #1780-01180, U.S. Government Printing Office.

Other ALA Publications for School Library Media Personnel

Educational Media Selection Centers:
Identification and Analysis of Current Practices
ALA Studies in Librarianship no. 1
John Rowell and *M. Ann Heidbreder* $4.50
Contains an introductory section summarizing the initial study and describing the needs which prompted it, the role of the National Book Committee, the purpose of Phase I, and the program itself.

Guide to the Development of Educational Media Selection Centers
ALA Studies in Librarianship no. 4
Cora Paul Bomar, program director; *M. Ann Heidbreder* and *Carol A. Nemeyer,* program coordinators $5.00
Contains an overview of an educational media selection center, including the rationale for such centers in relation to contemporary and projected trends in curriculum and instruction.

Influencing Students toward Media Center Use:
An Experimental Investigation in Mathematics
ALA Studies in Librarianship no. 5
Ron Blazek $6.50
An experienced teacher and school librarian shows how students may become users of the media center in an experiment with junior high school mathematics classes. The study carefully identifies the responsibilities of teachers, media specialists, and administrators in creating a viable learning program supported by the school's media center.

Instructional Design and the Media Program
William E. Hug $6.50
Establishes a foundation for organizing a school media program and coordinating it with the curriculum.

Occupational Definitions for School Library Media Personnel
School Library Manpower Project
American Association of School Librarians, ALA $2.00
Comprehensively answers the question, "Who should be doing what in school library media centers?"

School Library Personnel:
Task Analysis Survey
School Library Manpower Project
American Association of School Librarians, ALA $2.00
This report of a national survey identifies the tasks presently performed in over 600 outstanding building-level programs in the nation's schools. The questionnaire, *Task Analysis Survey Instrument,* is available for $1.00.

Services of Secondary School Media Centers
ALA Studies in Librarianship no. 2
Mary V. Gaver $5.00
Analyzes and compares the deficiencies and strengths of media programs in fairly typical secondary schools.

Steps to Service:
A Handbook of Procedures for the School Library Media Center
Mildred L. Nickel $4.50
Designed to provide immediate help and guidance to inexperienced and beginning professionals as well as a review for experienced professionals seeking to re-evaluate the school library media center program.

Total Community Library Service
Guy Garrison, editor $5.00
Presents the results of a conference, jointly sponsored by ALA and NEA in May, 1972, which attempted to clarify the concept of, and make suggestions for, coordinating library and education services to a community.

All published by
AMERICAN LIBRARY ASSOCIATION
50 East Huron Street, Chicago, Illinois 60611